NO MORE
TO NEED

Marilyn

Loving your love for Life

Thankyou for sweet music

coming from under

the trees —

Enjoy

Blessings & Namaste, always...

Deed Hardin

NO MORE TO NEED

POETRY
BY JILL HARDIN

Library of Congress Control Number: 2008902508
ISBN: Hardcover   978-1-4363-2965-1
                  Softcover   978-1-4363-2964-4

To order additional copies of this book, contact:
Xlibris Corporation
1-888-795-4274
www.Xlibris.com
Orders@Xlibris.com
47101

To my family and friends
and all sentient beings.

May all be healed
by the Beauty
they behold.

Contents

ACKNOWLEDGMENTS

I heartily thank and appreciate so very many who've given me this work to do. Their very words of appreciation and enthusiasm have spurred me on to publish these pieces that, of my innermost being and seeing have joyfully come about. My prayer is that they lift and serve the hearts and souls of whomever they manage to reach through these pages.

I would like to mention and thank first of all my parents, Mollie and Hal Hardin, who may not have always understood, but whose love pulled me through time and again. Along with that, my brothers Jan and Tim, whose love I've always felt and enjoyed. Right up there with these are my soul friends and teachers, more than I can list here, but they know who they are. I will say right now, however, thank you ALL so very very much for your never ending support, wisdom, vision, and belief you've given me. This includes many people I've not seen for decades, but will never forget . . . for they too are part of who I am.

And just as much, I want to say how very fortunate I am to be acquainted with my two beloved, wise, and beautiful daughters, Mary Neonta and Molly Rosalee, who've always believed in me, and encouraged me strongly and lovingly without fail. Last, and far from least, is my sweet beloved husband, Richard Munger, who quietly stands by in the wisdom of the Tao, and lets it all happen. Thank you, precious sweethearts of my life, thank you, for being who you are.

Pattie Anderson, thank you so much for your artistic inspiration and design for the cover of this book. I am truly pleased and honored.

And lastly, I must say a word of thanks and appreciation for the work Xlibris has done, and still does, to keep me on task, and guide me well through this wonderful experience of putting together, and out into the world, my first published volume of poetry. I may not have done it without them!

And thank you, readers and lovers of the poetic approach . . . be you blessed, at least once or twice, herein.

Namaste, all . . . . jill

The birds I heard today,
which, fortunately, did not come
within the scope of my science,
sang as freshly as if it had been
the first morning of creation.

Henry David Thoreau

A MOMENT OF GOLD

Isn't it amazing
  when the muses
    fill our gaze upon the world
      with lovely thought?

Or is it we
  who find the muses
    grazing
      in our fields of Bliss
    caught
      by moment's metaphor—
    Grace's gift
      by which we're taught?

Whatever the reason
  for the rhyme
  I thankfully take the precious time
  to seize these gifts
    and give them back
      in ways that lift
        the ones who lack
          for now
        the vision
          to behold them.

Be they blessed when these are told—
  for in each one
      a moment of gold.

AGAIN, NEVER THE SAME

This morning
 You sent me
   Pink Clouds
    again ~
  not the same
  never the same.

This time
  Half Moon takes center
     watching with me
         White.

Pink whispers
    in Your Light
      changing now
  to White chiffon
       swirling
     Sunlight
    reaching
       our favorite Dune
        dancing.

Ever New
  Beauty
      to notice
        or not
      ponder
        or not
  You send me.

    Thank You ~

        Every Morning   I Thank You
          for this Sky!
          as do
          these Birds
          flying
          upstream.
          Oh, My! How I Love Thee.
          Oh, My!

AND NOW THE FOG

Why would I not Kiss the Ground?
God does every day—
    with Sun, Moon, Stars
      Sky, Wind, Rain—
        and now the Fog!
      making tall black phantom
        of fall green cedar
          while kissing it!

Her roots must tingle
      to His kiss
    upon
      her glorious body of Life
        while suckling rain and food
          from our Mother's reservoir
            of Gifts.

In Truth
    her very Being
      is
the wondrous Gift itself~
    to oh so many
      other Beings
        seeing her this way~
all of whom
    are kissed by God
      as One
      Every Day.

EAGLE

Eagle
sits
on highest limb
Strong
Solo
looking out over
this small portion
of her Vast
domain.

Unruffled
by her hecklers
she will
move on
when ready.

ECLIPSE

MOON
    FULLY
        CAUGHT   in Shadow
                        of beautiful Earth
    sees Earth
        as Black Hole
                with Flaming Red Aura.

From Moon's perspective
            and she is Wise
        she warns
            of how
                we suffer
            our own greed's misery
                breeding
                the loss
                of Love
            and what is Simple.

OUR MOTHER
    so yearns
        instead of hell
    to harbor
        Heaven.

BUT A SINGLE HAIR

I am
~ as are we all
each ~
but a single hair
among ten thousand
on God's paint brush
for truth
through Beauty.

We have been
dipped
into
Clear White Light
the color
of All colors
as One.

We are carried
by
God's stroking Hand
forever dripping
with
This White Light ~~ Love ~~
to Beautify
All sentient Beings
and things
in this Sacred Life . . . .

The Beauty
    takes care of itself
      as long
      as there is Love ~~

      and there is Love ~~
    we need only
      recognize
        receive
          and pass it on.

I am
  truly grateful
    deeply honored
      to be
        this single hair
        moved by God
        in parallel
        harmony
          with all ten thousand
          of the One.

With humble reverence
  I smile
    at God
      and what we do here . . .
      this Love . . .

My Heart is glad.

  Tears of Joy
    gather
      and fall into it . . .
      this growing pool
      of Gratitude.

HER MAJESTY,
THE QUEEN OF THE SCENE

A slave to Beauty am I
　devoted
　　stopping at every sight of Her
　　　drinking Her in
　　　　savoring
　　　　　longing to hold Her.
　I'm a fool
　　a lover
　　a guardian
　　　for Her Majesty
　　　　the Queen of the Scene—
　　wherever I look
　　　I see Her!
　　Gasping, startled . . . and taken by Her
　　and Loving to be in Love with Her
　　　I breath Her
　　　　feel Her
　　　work Her
　　　　　water Her
　　　　feed Her
　　　　　　groom Her
　　　　　arrange for Her
　　and Thank Her—

　　all in the luscious act of Receiving Her!
I love Her so much—
　　I am a glutton for Beauty.
　　　　Thank　God　She is Everywhere!

HOW LUCKY THE BIRDS TODAY

Oh Great Mother
   thy vast lush body Gaia
      God's Gorgeous Earth Gem
   changing slowly with all of Life . . .

While we tiny wanderers
   complain and moan upon your back
      aches, pain, grief, rage
   of ever onward growth and age—
        You seem such
          Solid
            Sturdy Stoic
          Support
              under tired sore bones
                  and feet

          Until
            Suddenly
        Once
            in a Blue and Terrifying Moon
              YOUR creaks and groans
                SOUND themselves
                  in
              MOST THUNDEROUS of THUNDER
              under
            Suddenly humbled foot bones
              running
            from what feels
          Your Worst of Wrath!

Oh . . . how lucky the Birds today . . . .

Ah, . . . but no, this is not wrath
            which comes
            from You our Ancient Mother—
    t'is only YOUR Tired Bones
            needing
                to Groan
                    Move
                        Shift a little!

Thank You God, and awesome Gaia
        for being as Gentle
                as you were
                    for us
                this time around . . . .
        May we
    increasingly
        Heed
your warnings
    regarding
our disregard
for Your needs.

        Amen.

BRING THE THUNDER!

This storm
has pended
too long.

These waters
lie
deceivingly still.

Murky currents
rage wrestless
under

silent silken surface
becoming
gray dead gloom.

Bring the Thunder!
Flood the Fury!
Bury no more the Doom.

FOR THIS I'LL KEEP ON DANCING

No Dream do I remember on waking—
    only floating
        on suspended stillness
    still
            awaiting
                    the Vivid Dream Sought.

My Breath
    so still
suspended—
        I must Breath more deeply—
            Breath   in   Spirit
            lest it leave me
            completely.

        Suppressing Breath
            leaves Spirit outside
            awaiting entry,
                invitation.

        This heavy effort to breathe
            with furrowed brow
            and dripping tear,
                bring to mind
            the making of mask—
            heavy gut and solar plexus
                hurt Heart inside
            where things pile up
        in non-specific clumps
            of dark drab shape
                with   no   handle.

PICK UP MY BONES
off the Drumming Ground!
Get ready for the Dance!
Let Water gently float me into
Ceremony's Edge
where
Skeleton Woman's Spirit
arrives
just   in   time.

Breath me up
out
into
Holy Love of LIFE again—
Dance my limbs
move my gut
spin my Soul
into power place—
Move me.

Bones clacking on my Heart
lean me over
shake me down
lift me up
rattle me—

Expel these dark drab clumps
   that clog
      the River of my Life.
  Sift down the silt
    till it becomes
        the Clay and Rock Foundation
        deep beneath
          my Crystal Waters
            flowing Freely
          Thankfully exuberant
          unshackled
            and with purpose.

For this
  I'll keep on dancing.
    Muscle and Bone
    Spirit and Soul~~
    the Dance has just begun again!

MY VISION AND PURPOSE

I am a tall and beautiful
    Tree of Life
      flowing
        with grace
          exhilaration
            and   whimsy!

My deep Roots
    of Truth and Knowing
      hold
      in Sacred Stillness
      this Golden Core
      my rod and staff
        of Strength
          Courage
            and Wisdom
        while
these Radiant Branches reach out
    in Joyful Gratitude
      for
    Sun Moon Stars
      Sky   Wind   Rain
      Dancing and Singing
      in Ecstasy
        with All Beings
      on
    the Sweet
        Holy
          Healing Breath
          of Spirit.

My Purpose? . . . .

to Broadcast   and Nurture

Seeds of Love

and Forests of Joy!

LITTLE FLY

C'mon
  little fly
    I am not your enemy.
Let me help you
    free you
      let you out
      of this gigantic
           box
              of strangeness.

I see
  there is much
    along the way
      here
      that interests you . . .
  but each time
    only
    for an instant
      before
  again
      off you flit
        buzzing
          and pushing
            at the window
              where
        the day
          outdoors
              invites you
          to be free.

C'mon
   little fly~~
      I've opened the screen
         and slid the slider
            just so you can flee!

Ah ~ but you don't see it
  ~ your eyes are on me
         and my knitting needle ~~
     Here ~ climb on ~
       I'll give you a ride!

      Woops! you fell off . . .

But now . . .
   you're walking
      in just the right direction ~~
         don't stop!
      just keep on walking!
  till you find
    that crack
      I left for you
        between window frame
           and open screen . . .
    ~ Yes Yes ~ keep on going ~~

      Whoosh!

      Bye~Bye!

Now THAT'S
   the best thing I've done

   ALL DAY!!

I helped the little guy out!

NO MORE TO NEED

Oh Silver Gull
    spontaneous sprawl
        on rock awash with waves . . . .

Your gray-white Wings
    Of skill with Wind
        no more will ride this Sky . . . .

Your Silver White Transparent Spirit
    Soars the Spheres
        in Freedom now . . . .

There is for you
        no more
            to need.

WARMLY WONDERING

I think of you warmly
wondering when
or why
you even would
yet
wanting the moment
where
you'll wend your way
toward
my wandering heart—

wandering
only
for one small moment
before
again
I think of you warmly.

PEACE, YOU SAID

Peace
  you said
    "All I want
        is Peace   in my Life."

"Oh Yes!" said I

  seeing you then
    as someone
      with whom
      I could be Peaceful

  ~ as so you saw me ~

  and so we decided

    to Love one another

  in a Peace
      which grows
        and grows

    along with our Love.

      Thank you, so very very much, my Love . . .

HER MYSTERY AND A PRAYER

For her Lover
and their Loving
she carries deeply
every day
her mystery
and a prayer:

Let us swim together
the dance of two dolphins
this vast ocean
of body and Soul
where
every infinitesimal Touch
of Tender
Yearning
becomes
a Sweet Simmering Fire
Swelling
within each moment's
Tiny Vessel
Verily containing
Eternity.

LOTUS AND LAKE

In her healing
she became
a Lotus bloom.

In his healing
he became
the Lake
holding her.

In their healing
she became the Lake
he the Lotus
and back
again
in cycle

till they were One~~
and Everything with them.

HAIKU FOR PARDON

Darling,
   forgive me cause
      for this rippling
         in our Peace Pond.
      I love you.

CUDDLES

The trouble
with being
a couple
is
the muddle
of mind
becomes double . . . .

BUT—

As long
as the two
will cuddle
a bunch
the trouble
shan't burst
their bubble!

YOUR SLIPPERS

This morning
I open
  the closet door
      to get my walking shoes
and there
  I see
    your slippers
      with your own
        unique
          footprint
      warmly pressed into fleece
        to hold
          and claim
        for cozy comfy
          your tired feet
          your dog tired bones
            from standing all day
            at the pharmacy—
        where
          not only feet
          but legs and body
            ache and swell
            and beg
             for your sitting.

Today
    is your last day
        there
        for a while—
    thank Goodness
    you'll soon be Home—
        where peace
            and healing await thee . . .
        the geese
        the river
            starling robin thrush and crow
        then moon and stars . . .

. . . and your slippers—
    I'll help you into them

and next trip
I'll pack them for you.

TODAY RED TULIP

Yesterday
     I looked with sadness
          at Red Tulip bowing
               limp
               down
                    below full rim
                         of upright stems
                         ten thousand yellow blooms.

You said
          perhaps
               it needs more
                         water.

I took it
          from the others
     trimmed and placed it
               in
          it's own clear vase
               with water fresh
                    and brighter light.

Today
          Red Tulip
                    stands erect
                    glowing crimson   sweet and solo~~
                         passion in her gratitude
                              awaits
                                   our happy gaze.

SLURPING

Rain soaked garden
   weeds
      weighed down heavy
        along with all the desirables
          waiting
      for the discerning hand pulling
              up and out by roots
        carefully dodging peonies
          strawberries
           azalea and iris
        all the pretty little violets
          covering
          wet ground
        everyone
             blissfully
                 slurping
exponentially increasing by the hour—
especially the weeds.

   I'll get out there today
      and start pulling
        with apologies
        to what is happening
           naturally.
   May my own design's
      desire
        for control
     be
        not
          a sin.

MORE EVERY MOMENT

Oh God
   my eyes always
      follow   Beauty
        passing by
    a pain   of yearning
      drawing tears
        knowing
     I am   Seeing
     once again

   again
       and again

  Your Face   Oh God
      again

Your Face is Every Where
   in   Every Thing

  the only way to touch It
     is to Yearn
       tears of Joy
      while
         seeing
    more
          more

      more
    of your Beauty
     every Moment
      of the Day . . .

BEAUTIFUL WOMAN

Beautiful Woman—
    how is your Life?
        facing window looking out
    bulletins posted in alley way:
        "Need a Job?"
            "Family Picnic!"
    "Make Where You Live a Paradise"

Beautiful Woman
    wondering
        which sign shall I follow?
        they all speak to me.
            perhaps only words
            perhaps only wounds
        being nudged once more
                with hope for Healing.

Beautiful Woman
    wavering ~
        as business façade exits
        with meeting adjourned
        and men watch your Beauty
                float out the door
            of morning Starbucks
                in Fremont . . .

Beautiful Woman
    I know you well~
        You hold the key to the hearts of men~~
        yet yours must not meet their gaze.

You hide your dreams
in the depths of your heart
daring not to divulge them
for Fear
of their tainting
by judges nearby.

Oh Beautiful Dreamer ~
my heart is bursting with knowledge of you.
my heart is praying your dreams to come true.
my heart is hurting with fear
lest be
your passions subdued
your courage drained
by lesser than true calling.

You will need more courage than had I.

May my praying
take and abolish for you
any such crippling of spirit
and give you
sufficient knowing and calm
that your Beauty
and Dreaming
become for you
evolve for you
unfold for you
in the Paradise You Are ~

Your Love.

MASKS

People coming, going,
     peering out
      each through mask they donned today~
some wear same
     from day to day
      never changing what they say~
some change masks
     from hour to hour
      hoping to find more power this way.

Some wear no mask
   their power within
     they live on love
      and give it always.
Some receive love
     then drop mask
others don't trust~
     move on—don't ask
Masks on, hurting,
     searching with lust
      they see not Love is Near
for painful preference of Fear.

SAVE WHEN SPIRIT

We women, so long silent
with each other
and our men,
of fantasy woe and whim—
On finding Truth
is in us all
one and same
there is no shame.

Delightedly
but cautious still—
seeing self in others—
we share these things
and slowly lose
the holding of Despair.

The Desperado
lives within
the mind of Everyone,
save
when Spirit
seeing Spirit
sets the Demon Free.

OLD WOMAN

Old woman
pushing forth your pouting mouth
to speak your mind
your mind so full of
decided
angry
chatter
muttering softly
to noone is there—

You are so alone
dear sad old lady
not really so old
yet terribly mad and caught
inside your mind—
a lonely hell
behind your scowling eyes
of deepest sorrow telling.

Once upon a time
you were
a mysterious and beautiful woman.
Then
you gradually gave up
all your dreams
trading them
for fear.

I'm sorry for you, Old Woman,
    for the strength
            behind your anger
Is it too late
        for finding your hurt
                for turning
                    seeing
                        healing this heart
            so that once again
                your strength will be
                    staunch
                        behind your loving –

        Is it ever too late?

    Feel your fears
    Flow your tears
    Find your loving
    Have your joy!

    Pour these out
        till heart
            is full
            to bursting
                once
                again!

MOURNING THE DEATH
OF MY DREAMS

I Cry my Life's Losses—
    unfulfilled Dreams,
    Unforgotten,
 well up in my Bulging Tears
 and finally

        painfully

            Break—
Running as River over Dam
        many Moons
    Softening
        the hard surface
            of my Mask.

Oh Dreadful Fear,
    Deadliest predator of my Soul—
        Dissolve into these hot tears you yourself have wrought—

Allow them to penetrate the Life-Rings
                    of this   thick Mask
    until the Softening occurs in Depth

Allow them to Transform you . . . me . . .
        with bright shimmering Light.

Become the Vision I need
    to See that my dreams, in dying,
            are only changing.

Become the Courage I need
    to Live the Dreams
            they are
                    more
                    Vitally
                    Becoming.

REAR VIEW MIRRORS

Oh what a pleasure
      to drive my car
and treasure how fast
      I can go so far—
cursing and whining
      at others . . . . who
just want to be
      first-in-lining too!

So every time
      I hear my outcry
         and boy! can I let it fly!
I remember same crime
      I too often try—
         and cannot tell a lie
            so I sigh—
"again you've shown me, Dear God—
and Thanks
      for the fellow human mirrors—
         I easily see myself in them
         and again confess
         my own bad pranks."

RAP SONG

Busy busy minds busy judging
busy minds—
judging
    when we could be
        noticing the signs . . .

The signs are all along the way
    asking us awhile to stay
        and read between the lines—
    the lines that judge us every day.

Read between the lines
    drop the whining and be kind
    we can realize happily
        with hearts realigned
        the life
            of our own sweet
            loving design
        If we recognize in Everyone
        the Truth of the Divine!

So let our busy minds be
    busy loving God instead
        loving God in Everyone
        loving God in Everyone
    ~~ the Truth between the lines!
        the Truth in all the signs!
        the Truth of all Divinity
            is that we're all Divine!

AS BLOOMING FLOWER

As blooming Flower
   dropping petals
      for new seed—
   dropping judgment
  opens heart
blooming Love.

BREATHING

Watching
  the river
    moving east
    then west
    and all
  the in betweens . . .

  the geese
  the tide
  the grass growing
    flower blooming
    clouds drifting
      changing
      disappearing

  the color blue
    becoming gray
      white mesh
        again unveiling
        blue ~~

and all the while
            the deer
        in green field
            grazing

        and I
            in our good house
                gazing

        as the day
            the tide
            the clouds
                breeze
                sun
            fishing boats
        come in
            and go out
        as I breathe.

A LOVELY LONG TIME

Sunrise today
　lasting a lovely long time—
　　I sadly left you
　　　cleared the dishes
　　　put them all away
　　　and here!
You are Still Happening!

Whenever
　there is still drama
　　in the morning sky
　　　the Sun is still Rising—
　　　　making His Entrance
　　　　for All
　　　　　to take note!

I will watch
　and enjoy the drama
　　smiling
　　　till it is over
　　thanking God
　　　　Beauty
　　　　My Friend.

Ah, what a Beautiful Day this Is!
　Nor will it be over
　　till Sunset—
　　　with yet more
　　　　Fire and Glory!

SLOW TIME

It's raining now
    it has begun
the rhythm of living
   now
     slows
       to watching winter's weather
   whether or not
     we're ready ~~
  it's time
    to slow
      way down.

Life gets slow
  for me to know
   what's real
   and what is not.

How I feel
and how I thought before
  has changed
   and not a lot
    has as much
     importance
    as
   the peace I feel
   when I am here
   Now.

COAT AND CROWN

I have come upon
    a place   and time
        in knowing life   and self
            where
            my coat
        the many colors
                it has gathered
            through
        so many years of
                now I'd rather
                look at this
                    now that
                and then come back
                to this
                    or maybe not . . .
My coat
    the many colors
        I have seen
        and worn
        throughout my life
        will change again
        and endlessly

I pray it be not
        drab, gray, and dead
            nor
    bright and silly either
        but
    an interesting hue
        containing
            all the colors of my life . . .
    the flares of red
playful yellows
    moments of blue-green healing~~

        a mixed up myriad
            of nameless shades
    with tiny flecks of Gold throughout
            shimmering my Life ~~
    shining my Age
crowning my Crone with the wisdom she's grown
    through living and giving her life ~~
        in loving spoonfuls   or passionate blows
            no matter~~
        she's grown ~ and given her Love.

A POET'S LAMENT

But to capture these thoughts
   wafting through my mind
like air
   sifting through hair . . .

   No pen in hand
   they blow in the wind
      away from here
         back to source—
            the caldron
              stockpot
                 alphabet soup.

   Letters and language
        dripping disarray
          from leadless ladle,
            they miss their cue
            to fall on page
           never to be read
          nor heard
          nor said—
       not yet anyway
            to my muses' impatient dismay.

Ah! but why worry and mourn?
    it will be said some day—
        someone   somewhere
            some way!

    But mine is a passion
        which clings to such seeds
            sown
        by creation's vision of form.

So I mourn once more
    and scorn my denial
        of discipline needed and missed once more
            as thought
            and words
            no pen in hand
                escape
            my memory
            . . . once more . . .

AH, BUT GRACE!

Gray morning
  graceful bird
    in great wet sky—
ungrateful in mind am I
    downed
  by human condition:
    thought—

    circular path
      pounding outward
      inside
      walls
    of my own head—

Ah, but Grace
  the Green lush Blessings
    from this great gray dome
      do Reach
      through my gaze
        into
        center
    of mental circling craze
      and lift me up
        out
    into
      spiraling highway
        Skyward bound—

And finally Grateful now
I travel here
with Spirit
spacious
lighter
and Higher than mind.

TRY THE OTHER LINE

Isn't it amusing
   when the muses
      come
      to stay awhile—
after our abusing of ourselves
   when they're away!

It must be our Angels
   come to play on
   and beguile us
when we're so compelled to muse
   and thankfully compile thus.

Perhaps instead of self-accusing
   when these muses are away,
      we could
         simply
            dial—no fuss!
         and get them
      on the Other Line—
   the one the muses Trust!

WOAHINK WATERLILIES

Woahink waterlilies
slowly open
on still water silk
mirroring trees
across
bringing them over
to this side
to embrace the purely pink
perfect petals
of this most exquisite flotilla
elegant brigade
for Peace
and Beauty.

Cheer Cheeeer
then
Tweeeep
of osprey rising
on baby hunter wings . . .
then congratulatory
parental Chierp!
Chierp!   Chierp!

Spelling these sounds
is a mystery far less marvelous . . .
but . . . can you sense
the wonderous excitement
of another morning
at Uncle John's Cabin
on the Beach
of Woahink Lake?

MY UTTER LOVE OF BIRCH

So often
    in my search for inspiration
    through mine eyes
    it is the white of lone Birch Tree
        or two . . . . or twenty-three,
    that captures me
    with Light
        held   and emanating
        bright

    like purity
amidst arrays of forest
    greens browns and grays.

So unlike others' shining—
        always casting shadow
Birch shines from within
    and shadows may
        or may not
        follow.

And as my eye is caught
         by what
      this lovely tree in winter
             dropped,
   I reach to find
      a paper thin
             of bark
             white fine-grain paper
         silk
      given me by Birch
         this day
         to write upon
         my Love—
      my utter Love
         for Birch.

PINK

Pink
  is the River
    in Loving her Sky.
She holds in depth
    for now
      His reflection
while escorting gulls upstream
            to the Pink . . .
  " Look!" she says
          "God's painting again!"
      the gulls "Oh Yes!
                  we've come to be in
                    the painting!"

  How constant the change
      now Gold
        now Yellow
          now Silver with Blue
        and the Sun
          glinting their Wings
            lights the field
              casting shadows
                of Freedom
                  dancing.

  T'was a brilliant Pink
          that first caught my eye
    Oh my God ~~ what an Artist
            You Are

and bringing so many Gifts
each day
wrapped inside
this constant Change . . .

Thank You again . . .
Thank You again . . .
Thank You again . . . Thank You . . . Thank You . . .

EVER JOY

Ah Sweet Silence
　fog of fall morning
　　kissing Trees
　　ground
　　　last Roses
　　　and
　　　black shining underwings
　　　of Crow's quiet flight . . .

wetting autumn humus gently,　still . . .

　　　. . . and now　　sudden Light
　　　of flaming Leaf
　　　　crimson orange
　　　　　glowing
　　through the deep damp browns
　　　startles me
　　　taking my breath
　　　bringing again with tears
　　　　this Joy—
　　　　Ever Joy
　　　　　　of Beauty
　　　　　　to my Heart!

Oh Thank you Heart
　　　　my Soul
　　My God
　　　　Thy Beauty
　　　　　is
　　　　My Ecstasy.

PORT TOWNSEND

Seagulls mellowing
  find hot roof
    for roosting down the sun.
 We sip beer
   on shaded veranda.

  Cool waters
    breeze us up
     cool us down
   while same silent air
     carries
    slowly by
   feathers floating

     as close to stillness
     as moving can be.

   And just below the roosting roof
     the children climb
      shoeless
      down
     warm gray rocks
     to water . . . . .

   Ah—
    Ah—
      the water . . .
        blessing us all . . .

SEDONA

Red Rocks
　　Regal
Sedona-named heights
　　where air
　　　　more easily absorbed
　　　　　lifts my Spirit
　　with cooler
　　　　lighter
　　　　　　cleaner touch—
Before me
　　stand
　　　　these awesome Monuments—
　　　　　　Sculptor?—none other than
　　　　　　　the One
　　　　　　　worthy
　　　　　　　of Worship.
Red Rocks
　　Rising
　　　　calling at sight
　　　　this Awe
　　　　this Wonder
　　　　this Need to Worship
　　　　　this Stillness
　　　　　this Grandeur
　　　　　　Beauty, Strength

Ever seeming same
　　　　while changing—
Essence
　　always
　　　　remaining same.
Omniscient Stillness, God.

VICKI

Vicki~
    my beautiful Friend
        Egyptian Goddess
            woman of warm Light~

    She is Divine
        in Knowing
            pure of Soul
      Her skin
         deep mocha velvet
      eyes
         dancing joy
            as they hold
               deep love's compassion
      Her mouth
        a beautiful Rose
          speaking
            eloquence
        of love and purpose.

    Always ready
        for next bend
            in Journey's path
            away from Fear
    Courage carries all she believes
            on shoulders Strong
              of Faith
              that
         Righteousness does Rule
            through Grace
             and Unity
              of All.

MY MOTHER'S STRING QUARTET

Every time I hear
playing
a beautiful
string quartet
    I cannot but think, fondly,
        with tearful pride,
            of my mother
                and her
            string quartet . . .

    these Four Gorgeous Goddesses
        happily
           fulfilling their passion
               for the muses
               who traveled
                   so profoundly
                   through
                   the likes
                of Beethoven
                  Haydn
           Mendelssohn, Schumann
           Debussy, Ravel
           Saint-Sean
                  and Bloch . . . .

Oh! Thank God
    for the gifts
        He sent with these men—
            and these men—
                for giving them forth!

And Mother's Quartet—
    First Violin: Mollie my mother—
        her sensuous body
          intensely huddled
            on chairs edge
          ready for every beat and cue
        while swaying
          inside the tones of beauty
           her sweet small fingers
            and their beloved bow
          so strongly carved
          from string
  and excellent-old-German soundboard—
          this violin
            luckily smuggled in
            after WWI—
            its destiny
              thankfully
              my mother's hands
              and her heart.

    Second Violin: Connie— cute as a button
          fully dedicated
            to family and home
        save
          for this
        most precious of time
             spent—
         with her soul
           the music
          and these lovely
            lovely
            musicians—
            soul-friends.

Then Roberta—matron-saint of Cello—
          deep soul
               holding in straddle
               her true love
               the music
          coming from   inside her heart
               through this faithful
                    stringed
                         body of wood—
               faithful
                    for the way
                         she held it
                         and stroked it
                         with finger, bow,
                              and exquisite touch.

And Gwendolyn—the Violist
          sneaking away
     from her Jehova's Witness
          hubby Jess
               just
               long enough
                    for some time
                    any time
                         with the music
                         and these wonderful women
                         who play their souls
                         with her.

These four women
        so strongly bound
        by music
                Great Music they shared—
I'll always hold dear
            my memories
            of arriving home from school
                at least once a week
        and there they were— hallelujah!
                their luring strains
                wafting
                    through
                    the walls
                as I tiptoed by
                        and around them
                in utter awe
                yet   not understanding yet
                the incredibly rich Gift
                    they were
                    to my life.

And always
        will I remember
            my strong soulful mother
            a lover of life
        and the beautiful music
            she loved
            to play.

                    Not only
                          did she do this so well
                          but she held
                          together
                          her family of five
                          with Strength
                                    Love
                                         and Purpose
                    while
                          she played
                                    all that music.

Thank you Mother—

       I so Love you,
           and all
       of what You,
and your Own String Quartet,
       have given me.

       I Love You Always,
           your own daughter—
                              Jill

PONDER RATHER THE SWEETNESS

Mother—
  Please
    Believe
      my sacredness
      my knowing
      my loving
      my choosing
        my Being.
  Empty not
    your turbulence
      upon my pondering—
    ponder
      rather
      the Sweetness
        in
        your own Heart's
          Deepest Place.

If you cannot find it
  lean your head
    upon my breast—
        just as I have mine upon yours—
    now listen
    to my beating Heart—
  climb under it
      into it
      find your own.

Hear us Drumming together
Drumming together
Drumming Drumming
Drumming for Peace.

I will hold you
here
in my Heart
for as long
as it takes . . .
I do so love you . . . for I am your daughter.

FAREWELL TO A CANCEROUS WOMB

My beloved Mother—
    about to shed
    once and for all
        at 88
    thy womb—

your body's held it proudly—

    through years of carrying,
            birthing,
        loving and nurturing
            all three
        of your beautiful children;

    through further years
        of clockwork maintenance—
            the monthly bleeding and cleansing
            of your Great Human Goddessness;

    through many after-years
        of Woman's change
            and ever changing roads
            in your very rich life.

Your Womb—
    this beautiful part
    of Life's Ecstatic Design!
        where
      the Magic of Creation
        was nested
           nurtured
              embraced in Love
        again, again, and again—
      for nine long months each time—
      as is the arduous and Glorious Plan
      for the Human Mother Goddess and her Offspring.

I want to thank You and Dad—
    your bodies, hearts and souls,
  but most especially,
      this day,
    Your Womb—
        for My Life
        and the Lives of my Brothers.

There's an image I see now
    in the cancer
    your womb
    now harbors—
        your womb embodies your deep Love
           trying to embrace
                your deep Pain—
        pain no mother
        nor widow
        can avoid—
           nor can she withstand for so long—
      and oh, thank God for the Joys
        that,
      but for the pain,
        are felt.

I want to thank Your Womb
        for containing this pain.
                . . . and you
            for letting it go.
    May your Living
        be ever
            so much lighter now,
                    happier,
                still full with love,
                    . . . and without
                        so much pain.

MAMMA, ALWAYS

Oh Mamma—

   You
     have been
        my rock
   here.

I didn't even know   till now   how very much I'd miss you.

   You
     were always
       here
         for me.

Thank you, Mamma—
   You
     whom I
       have fought
         so long
       resisting
         so stubborn and painfully
           your good sound advice.

For some of this I'm sorry—
         particularly
           the piano lessons.

You were so so right.
    . . . . and for the ways
        we could not see
          eye to eye—
            therefore
             feeling
              hurt and judged—
    but now I see
    we both
      simply
        misunderstood
        each
          other.

Yesterday
   You lay there dying
     when I saw much more of you.

Today
   as I begin to move
     without you anymore
     I find you
        inside every thought
    notice you
       in all I do
   feel you
      bequeathing me
         your most astounding strength.

    I'm knowing now
    that it was you
    who gave me
    flowers
    in my life.

I'm knowing now
that it was you
who dressed me
with your love.

I'm knowing now
that it was you
who carried me
carefully
all this way.

You promised God
you'd do me right
and now I see
you did your best
and nothing about it
is less
than good—
most of it
is excellent!

Thank you, Mamma.
God bless you now
through all the rest of your Journeying.

I pray
God will bless us
again and again
with the gift
of knowing each other

ever and ever more deeply.

I will love you always, Mamma.

CHRISTMAS PRAYER

Ah, my Beautiful Life!—
   Transform me
      again and again
         further and further
   Take these opinions
            aversions
         this false importance
   Strip my mind
      dip it daily
         immerse it
         into the Depths
         of my Heart

         where

      Floating
      on Clear
         Still
            Waters

      a Lotus
         trembling pink iridescence
         is holding
            ever so gently
         enfolding
            caressing
         the Truth
            Love
               God, our Soul.

May Mind
    Ever
      Be
        so Empty

          so Blessed
            so Graciously Enchanted

              Clear
                Peaceful.   Amen.

MUTT 'N JEFF

Yellow winter Willow
    well rooted
    in its stand
next to white Beauty
    naked Birch
    neighboring
      roadside farm—

    we drive by
      hearing Neil's beloved baritone
      singing soulful Schubert—

    then two Hags
      old Maples—
        roadside buddies
        looking like
        Mutt 'n Jeff in their crone state
        chortling
          at people
            in cars
              racing by.

Returning together
    from RiverDune joy
    back to Seattle
      family
      and friends—
We're quiet
    homesick already
      dreaming Real
    our future
    at RiverDune.

THE BALLET AT RIVERDUNE

RiverDune—
　Longing to be there
　　looking out that window
　　　where
　　the gulls' high calls
　　　announce
　　the Morning Ballet
　　　over
　Siuslaw's quiet sparkling current
　　as she moves
　　　strongly
　　　　toward her home—
　　Her Mother's Ocean arms.

The Ballet
　seems
　to celebrate
　　the near Homecoming—
　　a mile downstream.
　Joining in
　　are two Osprey
　　　singing and soaring
　　　　over
　　　Great Blue Heron
　　　　waterbound
　　　　　standing still, stalking
　　　　　then whoosh—
　　　　　　a crossing
　　　　　　　mammoth power
　　　　　　　solo grace

while little blue barn swallows
busily
flit back and forth
fetching food
for their darling young featherlings
who peep
nonstop
from under our eaves
with urgently wide open beaks.

This Ballet—to think!
It is staged
right out that window
Every Blessed Morning!
without fail!

Changes, of course
in choreography
props
lighting—
and occasional additions to the cast—
a gentle doe
and her little fawn
saunter by
for early grazing
in field
by the River
and later the geese and their goslings—
same feast.
or rain and wind
pounding
Dunes, River, and Field.

But the Seagulls
    are always there
        to announce it all
           while dancing!

And I
    in Awe
and constant Wonder
    watch
the constantly changing Light
    on satin folds
        of Golden Dune.

    This Dune
        is like
           a Loving Presence
           showing River
              the Way Home.

PERFECTION'S GRATITUDE

Last leaves fallen Red
Iridescence
now gone brown
warming wet
    the seeds that fell
      just in time
        before them.

Just as there is order
    here
and all of Life
    Knows it
    We
    go   on
making our days
    from morning
      through the night
from
    summer's fall
      through rainy winds
        frosty fields
    feeling
        winter's cold approach
and Knowing it is Good.

Knowing it is Perfect
    this Order
    we enjoy
    as winter drives us
    into warmth
    cozy
    homes

fires and beds
we are ever grateful.

Oh
may All Beings
Be so given
to this well of Gratitude~

Perfection
Seen
Praised
and Thanked
from such
a winter's comfort.

May All Beings be Well
May All Beings be Happy
May All Beings Be Without Suffering

Namo Buddhaya
Namo Buddhaya
Namo Buddhaya

And Oh my Soul
of God
may I
if suffering comes to me
choose
Happiness with Love
that
this Light
of Life's Divinity
will Shine
upon Itself in us
and Heal
the suffering of All
in answer to our Prayer.   Amen.

WINTER HAIKU

December rose
   pink with love
      of light
   and little bird
      in naked tree.

CONVERSING WITH GOD

Today, conversing with God,
Sweet Tiny Hummingbird—
We sing love songs.

BLOOMING

My heart
   is a lotus.
      My soul lives there with God
        blooming
      every day.

THESE HONKING GEESE

The Canada Goose—
    geese, really,
        rarely goose,
            thankfully,
    for if goose,
        terribly worn
            and lonely—
but these geese
    arriving in twos and twenties
    every blessed morning until
        there's maybe a hundred and two
announce themselves
    as they land
        in great honking exhilaration—
        a celebration it seems,
            for they have just claimed
            their spot on the field
            to begin
                their day
                of eating!

Having landed right on the spot
    their long black necks
    turn heads
    bill to bill
like two black horn-playin' pilots
    with big white smiles
    givin' each other
    high five
    sayin'

"Oh yeah! Fine landin' today!
we made it again,
baby!
Let's eat!"
and they do~
they eat
all
day.

And tonight
when sun's been down awhile
before too dark for take-off
each couple
on their own impeccable cue
will make
a running start together

honking

and take off,
upwind of course,

honking

then circle round—
always heading west from here—

and . . .

still honking!

We wonder
where
they stay
at night . . .

TINY HUGE MIRACLES

Walking
        for wonder
                outside,
my heavy eyes
    slowly land
        on a petal
                iridescent
                fallen onto sidewalk
        from its sweet pink rose above.
My eyes
        then travel
                        up to rose
        still glowing its ecstasy of bloom.

Seeing center
        of this rose
            I travel through it
            down
                through hip
                    leaf
                        stem and stalk
                to earth
                    root
                    and seed.
Then more seed
            does fall
                    from center
            as more petals fall
                    to let them.

My tears too
then fall
with awesome Joy
for seeing such a miracle . . .
Truly!
permeating
every moment
of our existence
are
these tiny huge miracles!

Let us be kind to ourselves
remember
stop . . .

notice them happening!

The gift
of ecstasy
inside
each miracle
is given again
through the eye
to its beholder.

Thank You, Thank You.

TRICKLING FOUNTAIN ...
MURMURING KITTY ...

Trickling fountain
    constant sound
        of water moving
            fills the air
                making pure
                    the silence
                        where I live . . .

Murmuring Kitty
    purrs in my lap
        as I sit
            feet over rising heat—
                her favorite place
                    in the morning—
                also mine
                    when called
                        by pen and paper.

Seeing now
    the early pinks
        and mauve
            to fill my feasting eyes
                to tears,
                    I am called.
            And now
                it's turned to flame
                    in only moments
                        from the pink!

The Glorious Sun
   is approaching fast!
      How bright the yellow flame—
      pure—no smoke
      just Fire
     of this magnificent Day
     has once again
     painted the Sky!

And now
   pure Light
      Breathing it in
     I begin my Day
      inside
this Blessed Brilliance.

Praying, incidentally,
     last night's frost
      took not
   my new primroses.
Let them gently be warmed
     by this
    slowly rising Sun.
    Thank You.

THE BEAUTIFUL PLAN

Winter Air outside my window
    hissing rain
    traveling through it
    on mission to Earth—
        wetting grounds
        setting up freeze
            so bulbs and seeds
            will pop
            in time
            to greet
        the morning Sun
        in Spring.

The Beautiful Plan
    that always works
    over and over
    round and round
        the circle
        of our Mother
            and her Seasons—
                her Reasons—

        we must take great Care
            so the Beautiful Plan
            will remain intact.

    Let it Rain . . .
    Let it Rain . . .
    Let it Rain for now —
The Beautiful Plan is unfolding!

YOGA

Peel down
　unload
　　good Grace
　　　my body
　　　　then my face
　　　give Opening
　　to news inside
　　　as body
　　　　bends my mind-hold softly
　　　gently slow
　　　　till more is told
　　　　of closer
　　　　　more important
　　　　　　things and places
　　　　　　deep inside
　　　　　　　to go—
　　　　　the goal is now
　　　　what tells me well
　　　　of what exactly
　　　　　is
　　　　Right now
　　　　　for me
　　　　　　and others
　　　　　　　flowing.

Ah—Ah . . . . so Good to Be Here Now . . . .

Softly

I hear
inside

consent

to be content
with what is now—

Here
the air
is soft
safe
sane
serene.
Silence brings me
quiet mind.

Here
my Heart
is Happy

feeling
Divine.

GOOSE GODDESS

Every morning
    when the Geese arrive
        announcing
      that   the morning has arrived

    the Goddess of me
    the Goodness
        attunes
      to the God
        and Goddess
    Goodness they are
      we are
        All are
            as One.

We women Know
          Understand
            Feel
      her Wings   pumping
      her Heart   pounding
      her Love   pouring
            over   her children
      her Knowing
        what she must do.

    This Goose
        is Goddess
          of her domain
      as are   we all
            of ours.

And the wonderful thing about it all
        is the Grace
            that it IS ~
                just IS!

            we are Here
                Together
                as One . . .
        ten thousand tiny essentials
            of the One
                    Beautiful One.

        We must
            always
            remember
    Why   we are   Here.

    We must   Sacrifice Everything
            to our Knowing
            to our spiritual Truth
            to the Way
                that preserves
                    our Integrity.

    Follow the Goose Goddess
    Follow the Way
    Follow the Heart with Wings

Sacrifice Everything to our Heaven on Earth
where the Knowing
hangs in
with the Tao
in the holy comfort
of Now.

And every evening
while announcing
that evening has arrived
the Geese   take Flight   into Sunset . . .

it is   truly so
that
goodness abounds
in this most
astounding
Oneness
we are . . .

PRAYER

Oh God   Truth
Bring me back
      down
       into my Heart
      Sweet   Pink   Lotus
      where You sit
        smiling

      lovingly
showing me what is True ~~

      Love

      tenderly
telling me what to do ~~

      Love.

Keep me here always
         seeing   from Here
        knowing   from Here
   being and growing   Here
        speaking   dancing   singing
        from Here—
          only Truth
          only Love
          only You.

Whenever I leave
        please
            bring me back quickly
                back
                    to my Heart's sweet Lotus
                    where
                        You and I
                            sit
                    as One   smiling
                        in ecstasy
                    with All Beings

                        One
                    in Love
                        with
            Our   entire   Creation.   Amen.

THANK YOU SAINT JOHN

My Grieving has ended
                at last
        at least for now
                and oh, I pray to remember
                        how
                I came to this
                        through
                such eloquent Grace
        ~ good gift of Saint John of the Cross
                in his "Dark Night"~
                Oh . . . .
        Thank you Saint John
        for the words
                        of your ecstasy
                have filled my Heart
                with White Lilies!

I will always
                be able
                to return
                        to my Heart now
                        Thy Heart
                where vast winds
                        fanning our fires
                are stilled
                        humbled
        by the Sweet Fragrance
                lingering there.

MARTIN LUTHER KING DAY

New Moon's light
pure
white
bright
then fading~
Sun's pure gold
takes hold~
then Day
today
becomes
this year's honoring of
Martin Luther King~

one of many Kings
of
Truth   and Love

who've been slain
by
Fear   and Hate.

Oh Can We Please
get this Space Ship
together . . . rearranged
for the Beauty Field
Love   Truth   God and Angels
Heaven on Earth . . .

Thank You for Trying
dear and great
Martin Luther King
for the Truth You Spoke
Still Ringing Clear
throughout all these years
of Hope
Good Hope . . .
Thank You, Martin Luther King . . .

ONE FLAME

The One Flame
Burning
in All our Hearts

Is

The One Light
Shining
All around

Is

The One Love
Healing
All Beings
and the World.

Let it Burn, Let it Shine, Let it Be . . . that we are Healed . . . . Amen

OUT OF THIS WORLD I OFTEN WISH

In this world am I.
Of this world sometimes, mostly not.
Out of this world I often wish
    but for the times
        my purpose here
            becomes through loving clear.

Love the Flower
    Love the Stone
        Love the Mother
            down to Bone
                Love the Night
                dark, sweat
                Love the Light
                the chill
                the time it takes
                the waiting
            Love it
        Patiently with Faith
            watching
                musing
                    Knowing
    Goodness here is Now
        and there is Everywhere
            in Everyone
the Love we Love to Love
        the Love we Love to Give
                the Love we're Here to Live